Old MONTROSE

by

Tom Valentine

In one of the town's many parades, this vehicle won first prize. Paton's Mill is in the background.

ISBN 1 84033 010 4

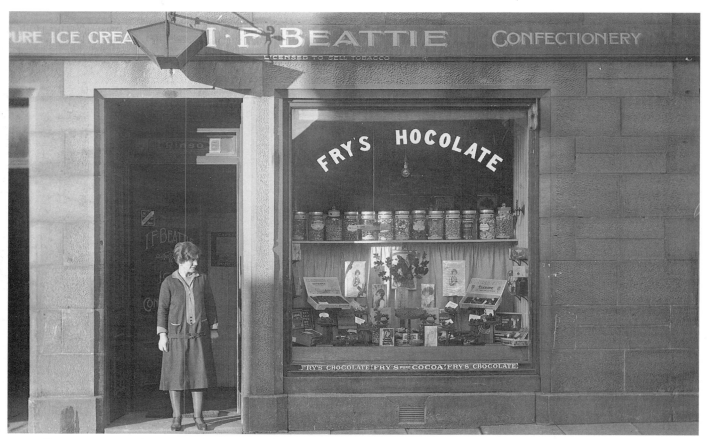

Beattie's sweetie shop was in business between 1928 and 1944. The premises were more recently used as a laundry.

The High Street wasn't always as wide as it is today. Until the mid-eighteenth century a row of houses ran up the middle from the Town Hall to the North Port so that, in effect, there were two streets running the same route. Many of the old houses on High Street are distinctly Flemish in design and it is likely that the town's trading connections with the Low Countries across the sea influenced the architects who designed them. Indeed, the steeple's largest bell, 'Big Peter' was cast in Rotterdam in 1676 before being brought over to Montrose.

Montrose had the distinction of having Scotland's first lifeboat. In this picture a Lifeboat Parade is passing along Murray Street.

Mr Sharp occupied these premises at 118 Murray Street from 1907 to 1918. In the 1870s more tobacco was imported into Montrose for manufacture than into any other port in Scotland after Glasgow and Leith. Indeed, as a pioneer of tobacco and related industries, Montrose was the original manufacturer of the snuff box, before the business found a more lasting home in Ayrshire.

Mount Road, *c*1905. There was a darker side to the town's tobacco processing. In the days of the slave trade Montrose boats would take a circular route via West Africa and Virginia. At Africa the original cargo of goods would be sold to slave traders in return for consignments of slaves. The ships would then transport them to America where they would be sold for tobacco.

George Street at the junction with Baltic Street and Bow Butts, where public hangings once took place. The lands around the Baltic were a main supplier of flax for the mills but this was a seasonal trade which had to stop in the late autumn. Thousands of seamen used to spend the winter in the town, waiting for the Baltic ice to melt in the Spring.

The Mall, leading from Murray Street to Rosehill Road, is one of the finest promenades in the burgh. The swimming pool now occupies the site of the houses on the right.

Cameron the bakers subsequently moved from their shop here at the junction of New Wynd and Market Street to new premises diagonally across the road.

Council housing now stands on the site of this grocery store at 2 Shore Wynd. After the First World War the local council, like many others throughout Scotland, turned its attentions to overcrowding in the town's housing. Municipal housing schemes were planned and duly erected, although this, and other improvements, took at least a couple of decades to complete. Even in the 1950s people living in some older properties had only a single sink and no inside sanitation.

REGETTA. MONTROSE.

Wharf Street, c1912. The suspension bridge was originally completed in 1829 to replace a dilapidated wooden construction. The new bridge was a source of great pride to the town but not too long after it was opened it suffered two accidents. In 1838 a supporting chain collapsed and killed a number of people who had gathered to watch a boat race and on another occasion about two thirds of it were torn up and destroyed by a gale.

LAUNCH OF THE "BAN HONGLIONG"
MONTROSE.

The source of commerce and trade for Montrose always came from its position on the sea. Shipping and ship-building were for long principal in the town's business. Possibly the peak of the town's involvement in these areas was around the mid to late nineteenth century. The town's boat builders mainly produced fishing boats but the harbour was also used by the Navy who brought boats in for repairs at the wet dock. An Admiralty report of 1850 commended it as the largest dock (and hence the most useful) of its kind on the eastern coast of Britain, save for Dundee.

The 1905 YMCA building now stands on the site of the old Lithouse building where dyers worked until the mid-nineteenth century. At that time Montrose's principal industry was flax-spinning and weaving. Other concerns over the decades have been whisky distilling, the flour mills, and rope and sail manufacturing. This century Chivers Hartley's jam factory has been and gone, but still in business are Glaxo the pharmaceuticals company.

The opening of the Traill Drive, 1912.

TRAILL DRIVE, MONTROSE, APPROACH TO GOLF COURSE

Traill Drive in the 1920s with James Winton's golf club manufactory strategically placed *en route* to the golf course. Winton & Co., as they finally became, were best known for their popular 'Diamond' brand of club which was produced from 1900 to 1939.

"Traill Drive," Montrose

Traill Drive, c1912. As a resort, Montrose came into its own towards the end of the nineteenth century with the expansion of the railways. This coincided with the decrease in foreign trading and Montrose became an elegant and douce seaside town.

STARTING TEE AND SHELTER, MONTROSE GOLF COURSE

Golf has long been popular in Montrose. The town's first club was established in 1556 and by the nineteenth century the course was known as one of the best in Scotland.

MONTROSE FOOTBALL CLUB
1921-22 QUALIFYING CUPHOLDERS 1921-22

WON BY
MONTROSE
1921-1922

Glory days!

On the beach, *c*1915. The sands were always a source of pride to the town and a great attraction to visitors. A writer of the 1870s waxed lyrical, describing them as a 'beach of pure sand, dipping at so fine a gradient beneath the wave, and affording so smooth a carpeting for the feet as to allure even the most timid to the luxury of sea-bathing'.

The Lifeboat Station, *c*1904. Montrose was also the home of Arbuthnott & Son who built lifeboats for passenger ships throughout the world.

LAUNCHING THE LIFEBOAT

An Edwardian photograph by local man J.G. Brown.

Paton's Mill, c1920.

Montrose Brick & Tile Works

The agricultural improvements of the late eighteenth and early nineteenth centuries, particularly that of draining wetlands, resulted in a nationwide boom in the manufacture of field drain-tiles. In 1826 the first tile works in Scotland was established on the Cessnock Estate near Galston in Ayrshire. Twenty years later tile works had sprung up everywhere. Dryley's Pottery at Hillside is thought to have been founded around 1859.

Montrose Brick & Tile Works.

Demand for field drain-tiles was so great that most works manufactured for a very localised market. At that time, roads were often in a poor state and the rail network was still incomplete so it was impractical to transport heavy goods over long distances. Hence many works also produced bricks for the local market. As the twentieth century progressed demand for clay tiles declined. There were fewer fields left to drain and plastic field-drain pipes were increasingly being utilised, decimating works like this.

Montrose once had two railway stations. This is the main station which was on the east coast North British line. The other originally belonged to The Caledonian Railway and served trains coming in from Forfar and Brechin, but closed in 1934. The competition between the two mighty railway companies was referred to in a local rhyme, 'The Caley was a railway of pride and great renown, The North British on the other hand was always breaking down.'

The Bents Hotel has been converted into flats and renamed Marine House.

Before becoming a barracks, this building was the town's asylum, built in 1779. At that time it was felt that there was a great need for a place to keep the town's lunatics. Normally, they were just thrown into the town prison where, as a writer of the time recorded, their 'disorders increased and (they) often exhibited the most shocking scenes of blasphemy and desperation'. A new asylum was built at Sunnyside in the mid-nineteenth century and the original building went into the hands of the Angus and Mearns militia.

ROYAL FLYING CORPS. DYSART AERODROME, MONTROSE.
" TUNING UP."

Dysart, near Lunan Bay, was the original location for the Royal Flying Corps Aerodrome before it was moved to Montrose. It opened in February 1913, the first of twelve 'air stations' planned by the government. It soon became a major training base for pilots, not only from Britain, but also from Canada and the United States. In the run up to the Second World War many of the men who later made up 'The Few' of the Battle of Britain were trained there.

Army Aeroplane Disaster, 27th May, 1913.
Wrecked Bi-plane near Montrose.

The remains of the biplane at Lunan in which Lieutenant Desmond Arthur was killed in May 1913. The correspondent of the card on the previous page wrote, 'I wanted to go up in one of the flying machines, but they wouldn't let me.' Perhaps if he had seen this picture he wouldn't have been so keen.

The opening of an extension to the Montrose Water Works at Kinnaber, June 1912. The town's water supply was taken here from the North Esk.

1805. Dubton Station, Hillside.

The branch between Dubton, Hillside, and Montrose was opened as part of the Caledonian line in 1848. It continued to be used even after Montrose's Caledonian station closed and its terminus was simply transferred to the North British Station, by then part of the LNER. The length of the line was only three miles but in the 1920s there were up to fourteen return journeys to Dubton a day. This gradually decreased as demand faded and finally the passenger service was withdrawn in 1952. However, the line continued to be used for freight traffic until 1963.

The Temperance Hotel and general store at the foot of the main road, Hillside. The North British Railway built their own station at Hillside to the east of the hotel. Competition between it and Dubton was fierce but in the end Hillside succumbed in 1927.

Loanhead, Craigo, *c*1911. This building housed the Craigo Post Office until its closure in 1984.

Craigo Mill was a flax-spinning plant and also had machinery for finishing cloth, a bleachfield and a soda work. At its height in the 1870s, the whole operation employed around 300 people.

WHENTHE DAY WORK OVER.

Ferryden fishermen in Beacon Terrace. All that prevented Ferryden from becoming a mere suburb of Montrose was the South Esk which separates it from the main town and its one-time importance as a centre of the local fishing industry. Despite its contribution to the area's commerce, the more genteel folk of Montrose had a tendency to look down on their neighbours. A writer of the 1870s rather patronisingly described the people as 'a muscular, weather-beaten race; but they are gradually approaching in manners and dress to the dwellers in the burgh on the opposite shore.'

BEACON TERRACE, FERRYDEN.

Ferryden has had a long association with fishing, dating back to the seventeenth century, but it was not until the mid-eighteenth century that the industry really took off. Fishermen from Banffshire came to take advantage of the deep harbour and housing was built to accommodate this influx. By the 1850s it was one of the largest and most productive ports in the north-east and those villagers not employed by the industry worked on the vessels that sailed in and out of Montrose. The towered house at the end of the row was the village school built by the local laird in 1832. In a sense it was the first kindergarten in Scotland, taking in local children from the unusually tender age of three.

A delivery to the Esk Hotel, Ferryden. For generations this was run by the Calder family and in the 1920s was the village's only pub. This was not always the case, however, and the place had a poor reputation for responsible socialising. At one time there were over thirty places to buy alcohol and one pub, the Jock o' the Den, constantly invited the wrath of the kirk. The church, in fact, claimed a steadying influence on the town over the years and eventually the village was reinstated as a sober community.

Ferryden post office and shop at Brownlow Place. This was the village's principal shop and everything that was needed was available here, from bread and groceries to oilskins and paraffin.

Ferryden's decline started during the First World War as many of the men were sent to France. Those that remained faced competiton from steam trawlers and boats that used larger ports as their base. By 1928 there were only 94 fishermen still at work in the village, a huge drop from the 350 who plied their trade in the 1880s.

"Fare 1d 2d" COY FERRY-BOAT LTD N°5

In the centuries before any sort of bridge was built at Montrose, Ferryden was the ferry post that connected the town with the main road to the south of Scotland. It lost this significance as soon as the suspension bridge opened and the village suffered from the loss in business that the ferry caused. However, the village recovered within a decade, with fishing established as the main industry. Despite the bridge there was still a need for a small ferry, albeit nothing larger than this rowing boat. 'The Ferryden Ferryboat Company Ltd', as this concern was called, was mainly used by local girls to travel to the Montrose mills each day, but the ferrymen's business was often jeopardised by unscrupulous competitors who tried to move in on their patch.

40

PREPARING KIPPERS.

Preparing kippers at Ferryden. The women were in charge of processing the catch, also for transporting and selling it at Montrose and the nearby markets. They were well known for their sharp tongues, often vented in the course of their bargaining: 'Do ye think puir men's gain to toil their bodies and risk their lives the hale nicht an' gie fish to you for naething? Ye wid scrape the guts oot o' an auld grey cat!'

FUNERAL of Dr SCOTT - CRAIG.

The funeral of Rev. Scott of Craig Church in 1908. A previous minister of the church, built in 1799, was a Dr Brewster who wrote the parish entry in the Second Statistical Account in the mid-nineteenth century. At the time the parish was affected by a peculiar spate of illnesses, which he called 'louping ague'. Its sufferers were struck by a temporary madness which distorted their bodies and caused them to run about with amazing swiftness. When confined to their houses they even started to jump and climb the walls. Dr Brewster advised that the best cure was cold bathing, although he mentioned, somewhat mysteriously, that one case was 'remarkably checked and cured by terror.'

42

A small outpost in the Craig area, Dunninald was the site of the chapel of St Skeoch (or St Skae) who, according to legend, was one of the twelve disciples of St Columbus.

The farming and fishing settlement of Usan was first recorded in 1548, but it may have been established as early as the thirteenth century. A saltworks was in operation and to house the workers this single row of 28 houses was built in 1822 by the local laird. The tower was also built around this time and by 1835 it was being used as a station for the coast guard in their attempts to suppress smuggling. This 1910 picture shows the village as a still active fishing community but by the end of the Second World War the place was deserted and the houses are now in ruins.

CHRISTENING THE BOATS
USAN

'Christening' the new fishing boats nearby the Usan Saltworks, c1905. The village's fishing industry peaked around 1855 when about 120 locals were involved but from then on there was a downward spiral. Eventually, most of the fishermen moved to Ferryden for the convenience of a larger harbour and by the 1920s there were only five fishermen left.

Usan House, built in 1820, stood south-east of Ferryden.

A scene at the front steps of Usan House around 1908, looking for all the world like a BBC costume drama. Such wealth - in stark contrast to the widespread ragged poverty elsewhere at the time - prompted a contemporary cynic to pen, 'Both rich and poor alike/ Their nakedness display/ The poor because they must/ The rich because they may.'

These buildings, now demolished, once stood next to the main road to Arbroath. Lunan was the site of another ancient church, built before the Reformation. A monument there commemorates the martyr Walter Myln, a church minister, who, aged 83, was burned at the stake in St Andrews.